# THE WORLD OF
# HOLIDAYS

## Paula S. Wallace

**Gareth Stevens Publishing**
A WORLD ALMANAC EDUCATION GROUP COMPANY

Please visit our web site at: www.garethstevens.com
For a free color catalog describing Gareth Stevens Publishing's list of high-quality books
and multimedia programs, call 1-800-542-2595 (USA) or 1-800-387-3178 (Canada).
Gareth Stevens Publishing's fax: (414) 332-3567.

**Library of Congress Cataloging-in-Publication Data**

Wallace, Paula S.
    The world of holidays / by Paula S. Wallace.
      p. cm. — (Life around the world)
    Summary: Discusses how typical holidays are celebrated in Australia, Brazil, Egypt, Germany,
India, Japan, Mexico, Russia, South Africa, and the United States, including instructions for making
a recipe, craft, or game from each country.
    Includes bibliographical references and index.
    ISBN 0-8368-3661-8 (lib. bdg.)
    1. Holidays—Juvenile literature. [1. Holidays.] I. Title.
GT3933.W35 2003
394.26—dc21
                             2002191113

First published in 2003 by
**Gareth Stevens Publishing**
A World Almanac Education Group Company
330 West Olive Street, Suite 100
Milwaukee, Wisconsin 53212 USA

Copyright © 2003 by Gareth Stevens Publishing.

Produced by Design Press, a division of the Savannah College of Art and Design.
Designers: Janice Shay, Maria Angela Rojas, Andrea Messina.
Editors/Researchers: Gwen Strauss, Nancy Axelrad, Lisa Bahlinger,
 Susan Smits, Cameron Spencer, Elizabeth Hudson-Goff.

Gareth Stevens editor: Dorothy L. Gibbs
Gareth Stevens designer: Tammy Gruenewald

Photo Credits
Corbis: /Patrick Ward, page 6; /Stephanie Maze, pages 10, 11; /Charles Gupton, page 18;
 /Richard Cummins, cover, page 31; /AFP, page 35.
Getty: /Deborah Van Kirk, page 30; /Ryan McVay, cover, page 43.
Index Stock Imagery: /Rick Strange, page 14; /David Ball, cover, page 23; /Linc Cornell, page 27;
 /Fredde Lieberman, page 42.
SuperStock: /Steve Vidler, cover, pages 7, 19, 39; /Ben Mangor, page 15.
Additional photography by Campus Photography, Savannah College of Art and Design.

Illustration Credits
Hui-Mei Pan: pages 8, 12, 14, 16, 17, 20, 21, 24, 25, 28, 29, 32, 36, 37, 38, 40, 41.
Katherine Sandoz: pages 4, 6, 18, 22, 26, 34.

Printed in the United States of America

1 2 3 4 5 6 7 8 9 07 06 05 04 03

All over the world, people celebrate important events with dance and song, feasting and games. The celebrations can be seasonal, religious, or political. They may be ancient, such as the Egyptian holiday of Sham el Nessim, which is over four thousand years old, or they may be comparatively young, such as Independence Day in the United States. Many countries combine religious and seasonal holidays to celebrate a yearly event such as the beginning of spring or the autumn harvest.

Holiday traditions have traveled the world with people as they have moved from place to place, mixing the old and the new. Christmas celebrations in America borrow many German traditions, including lighted Christmas trees, caroling, and even Santa Claus. In Germany, however, Santa Claus is called Saint Nicholas, and he visits weeks before Christmas on Saint Nicholas Day, December 6. New Year's Day is a common holiday around the world, but not everyone celebrates it on the same day. It depends on the kind of calendar a country uses.

Some holidays are celebrated only in their native lands. Many countries, for example, have their own independence days or special holidays to commemorate military victories, such as Cinco de Mayo in Mexico. Everywhere, however, holidays are times when people find special ways to join their families and communities in celebration.

 **Note:** *Whenever you see this sign, you must ask a grown-up for help.*

 **Note:** *Whenever you see this sign, you will need to use a photocopy machine.*

# AUSTRALIA

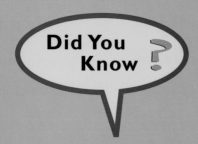

**Did You Know?**

**Over 120 languages are spoken in the Australian state of Victoria.**

**The Mars Murray River Marathon is the world's longest canoe race. Anyone thirteen years or older can enter. Held in December, this 404-kilometer (251-mile) race attracts over four thousand participants.**

The **Aussies'** biggest holiday is Australia Day. On January 26, the whole country celebrates the arrival of British Captain Arthur Phillip and the First Fleet to Sydney Cove, in 1788.

Annual events in Sydney include the Tall Ships Race, the Flags Afloat Parade, the Ferrython, and the Australia Day **Regatta**, which is the oldest sailing race in the world. The Great Australian Bite Gourmet Food and Wine Fair is held in Sydney's Hyde Park, and special exhibitions, gala performances, and concerts are going on everywhere. Spectacular fireworks over Darling Harbor and Sydney Harbor end the celebrations.

## Waterless Boat Race

In October, the dry riverbed of the Todd River in Alice Springs is the site of the annual Henley-on-Todd. This race is the original waterless regatta. Competitors climb into bottomless boats and carry them along the race course!

# How to make Nuts and Raisin Candy

**Ingredients:**

1 cup (170 grams) chocolate chips
½ cup (50 g) macadamia nuts
½ cup (75 g) sultanas*

**You will need:**
- measuring cups
- microwave-safe dish
- microwave oven
- spoon
- paper candy cups*

 Put the chocolate chips in a microwave-safe dish and melt them in a microwave oven. Be sure a grown-up helps you. Stir the chocolate with a spoon until it is smooth and creamy. Stir in the nuts and sultanas. Drop spoonfuls of the mixture into paper candy cups and let cool. Peel back the paper and enjoy the candy!

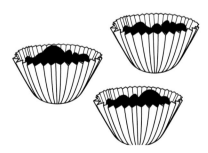

Sultanas are golden raisins that come from Australia. If sultanas are not available in stores where you live, you can substitute dark raisins. Paper candy cups are like paper muffin cups, but much smaller.

# BRAZIL

**Did You Know?**

From 1538 to 1850, the Portuguese brought African slaves to their colonies in Brazil, so Brazilian culture is a mixture of native Indian, Portuguese, and African traditions.

The dense rain forests in Brazil have flowers and other plants that grow nowhere else in the world!

Brazilians love Carnival (kar-nah-VAHL). This spring celebration comes just before the Christian season of **Lent**, which is a holy time of **fasting** and prayer before Easter.

In the United States, people in the South call Carnival *Mardi Gras*, which means "Fat Tuesday," because fasting for Lent begins on Ash Wednesday. In Germany, carnival time begins on January 6, which is the Christian holy day of the Epiphany, and "Fat Tuesday" is called *Fasching* (FAH-schin).

A central part of Brazil's Carnival celebration is a festive dance called the samba (SAHM-bah). Samba dancers and their schools compete fiercely to win prizes. Everyone takes time off from work and school to go to parades and to see which samba schools win the top prizes.

Costumes for Carnival range from huge, flowing dresses with large, showy headpieces and masks to tiny bikinis covered with sequins and feathers. The competitions, costumes, floats, and special drum music make Carnival a **boisterous** celebration.

# How to make a **Carnival Mask**

**You will need:**
- **scissors**
- **pencil**
- **cardboard**
- **glue**
- **tape**
- **wooden dowel that is 10 to 12 inches (25 to 30 centimeters) long**
- **glitter**
- **feathers**

**❶** Photocopy the mask patterns below. Enlarge them, if necessary, to fit your face. Cut out the patterns.

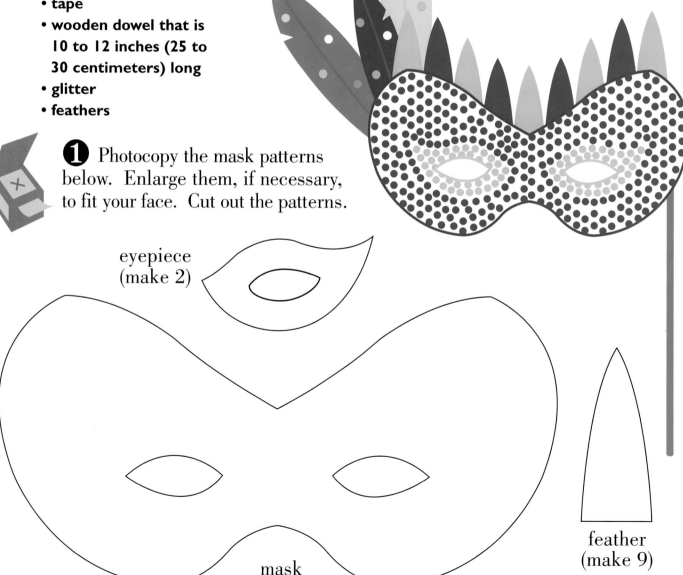

eyepiece
(make 2)

feather
(make 9)

mask

**❷** Draw around the patterns on pieces of cardboard. Cut out the cardboard shapes. Have a grown-up help you cut out the eyeholes in the mask and eyepieces.

**❸** Glue each eyepiece over an eyehole on the mask.

**❹** Glue the feather shapes to the back of the mask along the top edge.

**❺** Glue or tape the dowel to the back of the mask along one side.

**❻** Decorate the mask any way you like. Make a fancy bird mask, like this one, with glitter and feathers. You could also decorate the background, then add some sparkle. It's all up to you!

# EGYPT

Mulid el Nabawy (MOO-lid el NAB-ah-way) is an **Islamic** holiday. It means "birthday of the prophet." On this day, Egyptians make pink candies in the shapes of horses or dolls. They also dress up in their best clothes and decorate their streets and shops.

Sham el Nessim (SHAM el na-SEEM) is a spring holiday that Egyptians have celebrated for more than 4,500 years. In Arabic, *sham* means "smell," and *el nessim* means "air." *Sham el Nessim* means "smelly air" because, on this day, people traditionally gave offerings of salted fish, lettuce, and onions to the Egyptian gods. Egyptians enjoy the same kinds of foods in celebrations today. They also dye eggs beautiful colors to represent the new life of spring. Egyptians are believed to have been the first people to dye eggs.

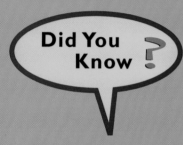

**Did You Know?**

The largest pyramid in Egypt is the Great Pyramid of Khufu. It covers 13 acres (5.3 hectares) and is made of more than two million stone blocks. They are not little blocks, either. Each of them weighs more than 2 tons (1,800 kilograms)!

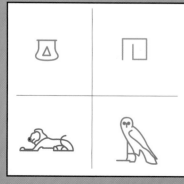

# Hieroglyphics

For four hundred years, Egyptians wrote in pictures called hieroglyphs (HIGH-row-glifs). Hieroglyphic writing can be read left to right or right to left. A reader can tell which direction because the figures always face toward the beginning of the line. Hieroglyphic writing can also be in columns read from top to bottom.

# How to write with **Hieroglyphs**

| a | b | c | d | e |
|---|---|---|---|---|
| **f** | **g** | **h** | **i** | **j** |
| **k** | **l** | **m** | **n** | **o** |
| **p** | **q** / **r** | **s** | **t** | **u** |
| **v** | **w** | **x** | **y** | **z** |

Use this shortened hieroglyphic alphabet (opposite page) as a guide to making hieroglyphs. When the same picture is used for more than one letter, the color of the hieroglyph becomes part of the code.

**You will need:**
• paper
• colored pencils

**1** Match the letters of words to the pictures in the hieroglyphic alphabet. Draw a sentence, like the one below, on paper with colored pencils. What do you think the hieroglyphic writing says on the next two lines below?

I    l    o    v    e        y    o    u

**2** Use the hieroglyphic alphabet to write a message to a friend or to sign your name the ancient Egyptian way.

17

# GERMANY

**Did You Know ?**

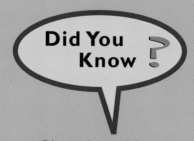

Gingerbread houses and gingerbread cookies come from Deutschland (DOYCH-luhnd), the German name for Germany. The story of Hansel and Gretel has a famous ginger-bread house that is owned by a witch!

Germans have a tradition of counting down the days to Christmas Day with an **Advent** calendar. Advent is a Christian holy season that begins four Sundays before Christmas. Many children count the days to Christmas on paper calendars that have a little door for each day or each week during Advent. The doors open to show a Christmas scene. Some Advent calendars are made of cardboard or wood with a piece of chocolate or a small gift behind each door.

German children have another little taste of Christmas on December 6, which is Saint Nicholas Day. Late at night on December 5, Saint Nicholas visits each house, leaving small gifts and cookies in the shoes of good children and lumps of coal for naughty boys and girls. Saint Nicholas is known and loved for secretly helping people. On Saint Nicholas Day we can all be "secret givers," which means doing nice things for people without letting them know who did it.

# How to make an
# Advent Calendar

**You will need:**
- scissors
- tape
- large piece of cardboard
- ballpoint pen
- markers or crayons
- hole punch
- ribbon

**1** Photocopy and enlarge the pattern of the barn (right), which represents the stable where Jesus was born.

**2** Cut out the copied pattern and tape it to the piece of cardboard.

**3** With the point of the pen, carefully punch small holes in the pattern along the dashed lines. The pen will make dots on the cardboard to show you where to cut open the windows and door.

**4** Cut the cardboard along the edges of the pattern, then remove the pattern.

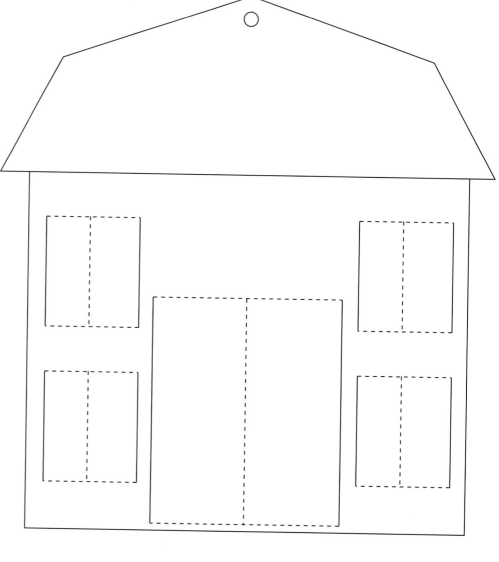

**5** Have a grown-up help you cut along the dotted lines so the windows and door will open and close.

**6** Decorate the front of the barn with markers or crayons. Choose a favorite photo or make a drawing or write a message. You will need one photo, drawing, or message for each window and one for the door. Tape them onto the back of the barn so they will show through the windows and the door.

**7** To hang your calendar, punch a hole at the top of the barn and tie a piece of ribbon through the hole to make a loop. On each Sunday during Advent, open one window. Open the door on Christmas Day.

# INDIA

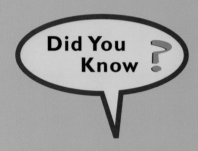

**Did You Know ?**

Indian women and girls get ready for special events by painting *mehndi* (MEN-dee) on their hands. Mehndi is the art of painting intricate patterns on the body with a dye called henna. The patterns are painted on either freehand or using a stencil.

In India, not a single day goes by without a celebration or a festival in one region or another. Celebrations in India are magnificent and extravagant. Most often, they are colorful and noisy, too. At the annual Great Elephant March, a hundred or more parading elephants are decorated with jewels, ornate saddles, and even festive umbrellas!

Diwali (dee-WAH-lee) is celebrated for five continuous days all over India. It is the **Hindu** (HIN-doo) Festival of Lights. Homes, shops, and offices are decorated with **neon** and strings of tiny electric lights, as well as with small clay lamps that give off a warm, orange glow to welcome Lakshmi (LAHK-shmee), the goddess of wealth and prosperity. Diwali is an especially happy time, full of feasting, gifts, and expressions of love.

Holi (WHO-lee), which is the Festival of Colors, announces the arrival of spring and celebrates the triumph of good over evil. People throw colored powder and balloons filled with colored water at each other.

# How to do
# Mehndi Hand Painting

In India, mehndi patterns are painted on the skin with a semi-permanent, reddish brown dye called henna. Our version of mehndi will easily wash off with soap and water.

**You will need:**
- pencil
- paper
- small watercolor paintbrush
- washable, nontoxic stamp pad, with brown or black ink if you are fair-skinned, gold or silver ink if you have a dark complexion

❶ Draw around your hand on a piece of paper. Plan your mehndi pattern on this paper outline. You can use the design ideas on this page or create your own designs. Use your finished pattern as a guide in the next step.

❷ To copy a finished design onto your hand, press the hard end (not the bristle end) of the paintbrush on the ink pad. Then press the inked end of the paintbrush onto the back of your hand to make a dot. Repeat this step to make each dot.

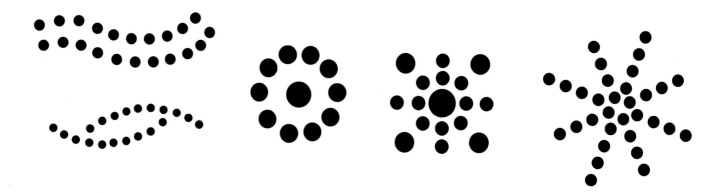

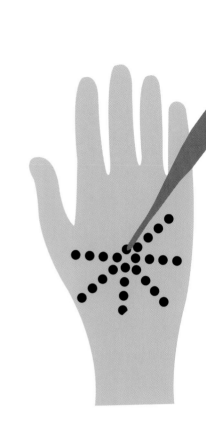

**❸** To make larger dots, press on a cluster of small dots, overlapping them. You might want to practice on a piece of paper first. To make lines, press on dots all in a row.

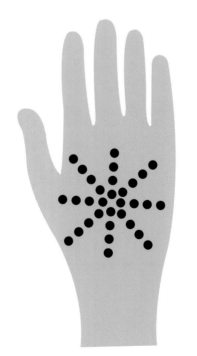

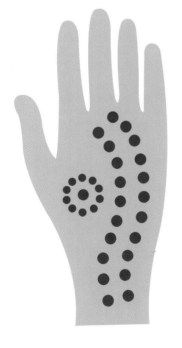

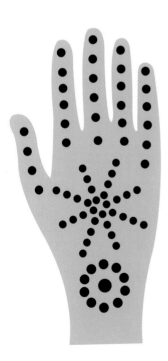

# JAPAN

**Did You Know ?**

During the traditional Japanese holiday of Setsubun (SET-soo-boon), people eat the same number of beans as the years of their age in order to have good luck and good health.  If, for example, you are nine years old, you would eat nine beans on the day of Setsubun!

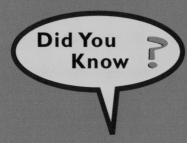

Jidai-Matsuri (GEE-dye-maht-SOO-ree), the Japanese Festival of Ages, **commemorates** the history of **Kyoto** (KEY-oh-toh). More than two thousand people, who are all dressed in native costumes from different times in Japanese history, parade through the city.

For Hina-Matsuri (HEE-nah-maht-SOO-ree), which is also known as Dolls' Festival, special dolls dressed in silk are displayed in a **shrine**.  A complete shrine shows an ancient royal family, including Emperor and Empress, three ladies-in-waiting, and five musicians. Girls have the important job of looking after the dolls and serving tea and rice cakes to guests.

May 5 is Kodomono-Hi (KOH-doh-moh-noh-hee), or Children's Day.  Boys display warrior dolls, swords, and a *kabuto* (KAH-boo-toh), which is a miniature warrior's helmet, and people hang **carp** streamers outdoors.  These colorful cloth kites are attached to long bamboo poles.  The oldest son gets to fly the biggest carp.  Younger sons fly smaller carp streamers.

# How to make a **Carp Streamer**

**You will need:**
- scissors
- paste or glue
- large sheets of brightly colored, lightweight paper
- large sheet of heavy paper, about 14 x 16 inches (35 x 40 cm)
- metal, plastic, or wooden ring with a 4-inch (10-cm) diameter (available at craft stores)
- crepe paper
- clear tape
- hole punch
- string

**❶** Photocopy the patterns below. Have a grown-up help you enlarge them so that the mouth and head pieces are approximately 14 inches (35 cm) from top to bottom. Cut out the enlarged patterns and paste them onto sheets of brightly colored paper. Cut around the patterns to make colored shapes.

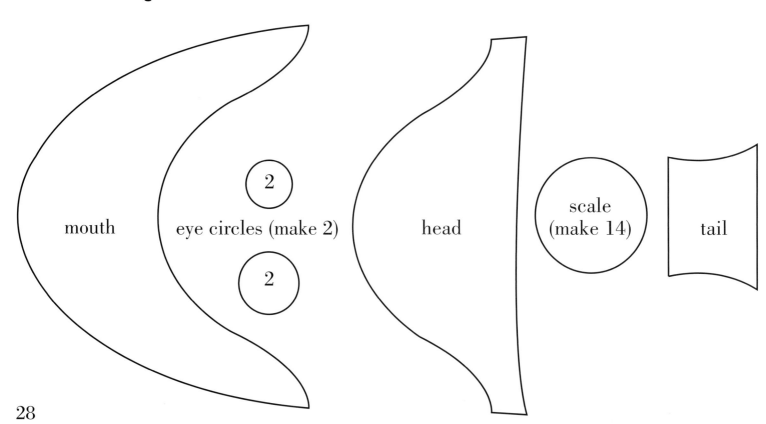

mouth

eye circles (make 2)

2

2

head

scale (make 14)

tail

**❷** Paste the colored shapes onto the large sheet of heavy paper. Paste the small eye circles onto the large eye circles. Paste the scales so that they are overlapping. To make them look more like fish scales, paste only the top part of each circle, so the rest of the paper flaps freely.

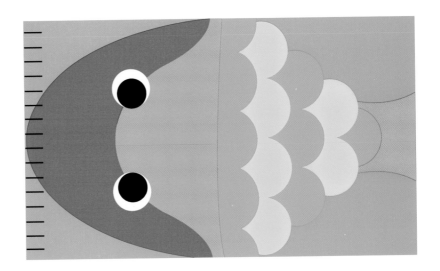

**❸** Make tiny cuts, about ¹/₂ inch (1.25 cm) deep, all along the edge of the large sheet of paper that is closest to the carp's mouth. Carefully fold the tabs of the cut edge around the ring and paste them in place. Now paste the long sides of the paper together, forming a tube.

**❹** Cut long streamers out of the crepe paper and tape them inside the tail end of the tube.

**❺** Punch a hole on each side of the tube at the mouth end. Thread string through the holes (as shown below). Hook the string to a fence post or a tree branch and let the breeze show off your carp streamer.

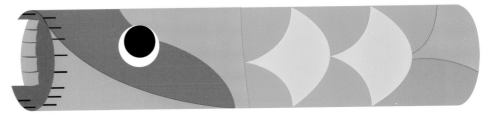

29

# MEXICO

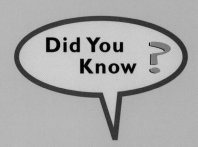

**Did You Know?**

*Cinco de Mayo,* (SEEN-koh day MY-oh), which means "Fifth of May," is a Mexican holiday commemorating Mexico's victory over the French in 1862. It is a day for celebrating courage and freedom, much like the Fourth of July holiday in the United States.

*El Día de los Muertos* (el DEE-ah day los MWER-tohs) means "the day of the dead" in Spanish. It is celebrated just after Halloween, on November 1, the same day as All Saints' Day. Mexicans believe that the spirits of the dead return to earth for a visit on this day. Rather than focusing on scary ghost stories, however, families set up altars in their homes and prepare food to welcome the spirits.

On the evening of November 1, families bring food to the cemeteries to leave as an offering to their deceased relatives. They decorate the graves with candles, incense, and flowers and pray for those who have died. Then they say good-bye to their ancestors until the next year.

To celebrate El Día de los Muertos, people sell jewelry and chocolates in the shapes of skeletons and skulls, and bakers sell *pan de los muertos,* which is sweet bread shaped like skulls and bones.

# Chocolate

Chocolate was part of the lives of the ancient peoples of Mexico. The **Aztecs** made chocolate into a drink by roasting cacao beans, grinding them, mixing them with corn, then adding vanilla and water to the paste. Because the cacao bean was used as money by the **Mayan** people, only Mayan kings and priests were allowed to drink or eat it.

# How to make Chocolate Skulls and Bones*

**Ingredients:**

²/₃ cup (113 g) milk chocolate chips

3 tablespoons (45 milliliters) light corn syrup

**You will need:**
- measuring cup and spoons
- double boiler or nonstick saucepan
- wooden spoon
- plastic wrap
- toothpicks

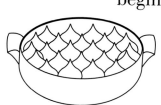 Put the chocolate chips in a double boiler or a nonstick saucepan over very low heat. Stir them with a wooden spoon until they are completely melted. Blend in the corn syrup. The chocolate will begin to stiffen right away. Scoop the chocolate onto a piece of plastic wrap and let it cool in the refrigerator for 10 to 15 minutes. When you take it out, **knead** the chocolate to make it easier to work with. Break off a piece of the chocolate and shape it into a skull or a bone. Keep making skulls and bones until you have used up all of the chocolate. Use toothpicks to carve the skulls' faces.

 For this recipe, you will need to make modeling chocolate, which is a soft, bendable candy you can form into different shapes.

# RUSSIA

Did You Know ?

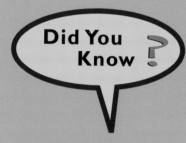

The world's most famous Easter eggs are made of enamel and precious metals and are decorated with gold and costly gems. They were made in Russia by a jeweler named Peter Carl Fabergé. The first Fabergé egg was made in 1885 for **Czar** Alexander to give to his wife, Maria. From then on, Fabergé made eggs each year at Easter for the Russian royal family.

Kolyada (kah-LYAH-dah) is an outdoor Christmas celebration in Russia. Children make snow ladies, using prunes for eyes and green beans for noses.

Maslyanitsa (mah-slee-NYET-sah) is a week-long festival of pancake eating at the end of winter. The week before the fasting of Lent begins, Russians enjoy pancakes with **caviar**, fresh cream, and honey or butter.

*Ivan Kupala* (EE-vahn KOO-pah-lah) is Russian for "John the Baptist." It is a holiday in honor of St. John the Baptist, and water plays a central role. Children spend all day swimming and playing in rivers. At night, boys and girls hold hands and jump over small fires. If they land still holding hands, people believe there will be a wedding soon.

Easter is celebrated with a feast that includes sweet round bread called *kulich* (KOO-leesh), sweet **curds** with butter, and raisin pudding called *pashka* (PAHSH-kah). The kulich has icing with the letters XB in it. The letters stand for "Christ is risen." The pashka is decorated with candied cherries in the form of a cross. Easter decorations include brightly colored painted eggs.

# How to make an
# Easter Tree with Painted Eggs

**You will need:**
- **eggs**
- **small needle**
- **bowl**
- **watercolors or acrylic paints**
- **paintbrush**
- **small tree branch**
- **container**
- **sand or small stones**
- **paper clips**

**❶** Before you paint eggs for your Easter tree, you need to blow the raw eggs out of their shells, so the eggs will be light enough to hang from the branch. You can blow out the eggs ahead of time, as you use eggs for cooking and eating, collecting a few shells at a time.

> **CAUTION!**
> Be careful not to eat any raw egg and always wash your hands thoroughly after handling raw eggs.

**❷** To blow an egg out of its shell, use a small needle to make a hole at each end of the eggshell. Because eggshells crack very easily, you might need to have a grown-up help you make the holes.

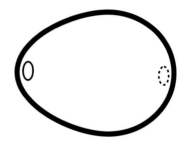

**❸** After you have made both holes, blow into one hole, pushing the raw egg out through the other hole into a bowl. Carefully wash the eggshell and let it dry. Store empty shells in an egg carton until you are ready to paint them.

**4** Paint the eggshells with watercolors or acrylic paints. Let the paint dry completely.

**5** Set the tree branch in the container. Put sand or small stones around the branch so it stands up straight.

**6** Open up each paper clip so it will fit through the hole in the pointed end of an eggshell. Carefully feed one end of a paper clip into the hole on each shell. The paper clip will work like a hook inside the shell to hold it.

**7** Hang the eggs on the tree branch for a colorful Easter decoration.

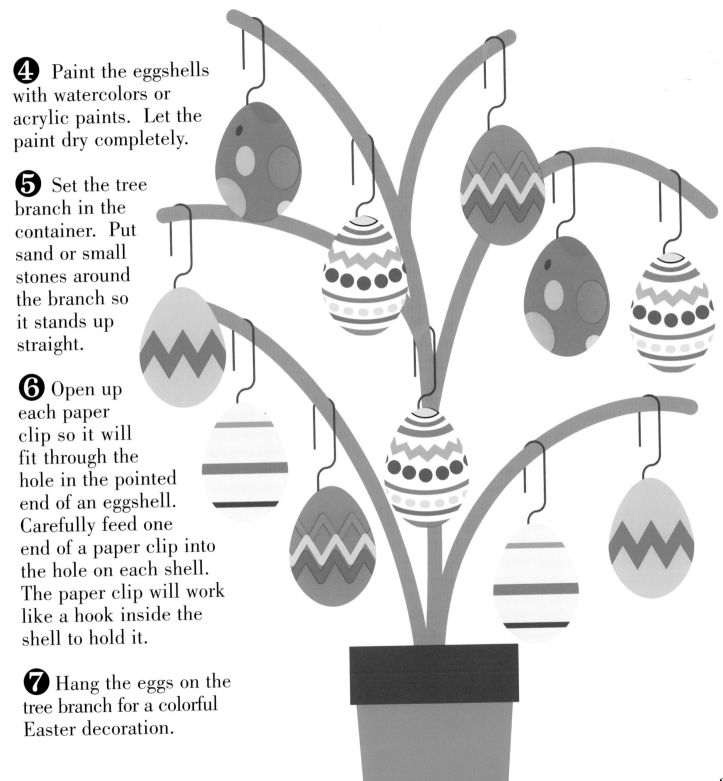

# SOUTH AFRICA

**Did You Know ?**

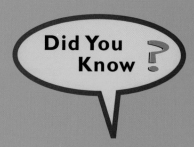

A nickname for South Africans is "Springboks." A springbok is a small, graceful antelope found in southern Africa.

South Africa has four major native tribes and many smaller tribes. As part of an effort to keep tribal culture alive, Johannesburg, which is a large city in South Africa, holds a regular folk show with children dressed in traditional tribal costumes.

One of South Africa's largest tribes is the Zulu. When Zulu boys are nine years old, they must perform certain tasks to be initiated into manhood and earn the right to be called one of "Those Who Have Heard the Bird." This title means that they have respect for the land and for their ancestors.

As part of the initiation into manhood, Zulu boys' heads are shaved, their faces are painted with red clay, and they are given a bracelet made from the hairs of an elephant's tail. Sometimes, a bull is sacrificed for this coming-of-age event.

Talented Zulu artists make baskets, carvings, pottery, and beadwork. Before glass beads became popular, Zulu beads were made from seeds, seashells, ivory, and teeth.

# How to make a
# Zulu Bead Key Chain

**You will need:**
- scissors
- felt
- hole punch
- pencil
- tracing paper
- thread
- needle
- beads
- glue
- key chain loop
  **(available at craft stores)**

**1** Cut the felt into two 3- x 1-inch (7.5- x 2.5-cm) rectangles and lay one on top of the other.

**2** Use a hole punch or your scissors to make a small hole at one end of each felt rectangle for the key chain loop to go through. Set one felt rectangle aside. It will be attached later.

**3** Use the design pattern below or make up your own design. To use the pattern below, trace the design onto a sheet of tracing paper.

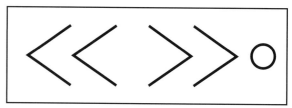

design pattern on tracing paper

**4** To transfer the design onto the felt, place the tracing paper over the felt and punch little dots through the tracing paper with a sharp pencil. You will use the dotted lines on the felt as a guide for sewing on the beads.

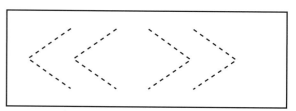

design transferred onto felt

**❺** Thread the needle and knot the end of the thread. Starting from behind the felt, push the needle up through the felt at one end of the design pattern. Put two beads on the needle, then push the needle back down through the felt.

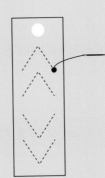

**❻** Following the dotted pencil lines, continue to push the needle up and down through the felt, adding two beads with each stitch.

**❼** When you have covered all of the pencil lines with beads, push the needle down through the felt to the back side. Cut the thread close to the needle and tie a knot in the thread.

**❽** Glue the second felt rectangle onto the back of the beaded rectangle. To hold the two pieces of felt together more securely, you can stitch around the edges of the felt. Using thread that is a contrasting color will make the key chain even more decorative.

**❾** Put the key chain loop through the holes in the felt rectangles. Now, just add keys!

# UNITED STATES

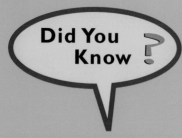
Thanksgiving is similar to a Jewish harvest celebration in autumn called Sukkot (soo-KOHT), a Hebrew word meaning "booth." The booth symbolizes the temporary shelters that protected the ancient Jewish people during their forty years in the desert.

Sukkot booths must have three sides, and you must be able to see the stars through the roof. Children decorate the booth with paper chains and hanging fruit.

People in the United States celebrate the founding of their nation on July 4, which is the day the **Declaration of Independence** was adopted in Philadelphia in 1776. Fourth of July celebrations usually include parades, picnics, and fireworks.

Thanksgiving, celebrated on the fourth Thursday in November, is another important holiday in the United States. People try to spend this day with their families and friends, sometimes traveling long distances to be together. The Thanksgiving tradition began in 1621 in Plymouth, Massachusetts, when the **Pilgrims**, who were English settlers, joined Native Americans in a feast to give thanks for the autumn harvest and for surviving the year.

At the first Thanksgiving, the Pilgrims and the Native Americans shared roasted wild turkey and **venison**. Turkey is still the center of traditional Thanksgiving meals. Other traditional foods include corn, cranberries, and pumpkin pie.

# How to make a
# Pinecone Bird Feeder

With days getting colder and winter approaching, autumn is a good time to help the birds in the yard find food to eat. Autumn is also a lovely time to go for a walk. On your next walk, gather some pinecones. Then, when you celebrate the autumn harvest feast of Thanksgiving, you can include the birds in your celebration by making them a pinecone bird feeder.

**You will need:**
- **old newspapers**
- **piece of string, yarn, or wire that is 3 feet (1 meter) long**
- **one large pinecone**
- **Popsicle stick, plastic knife, or putty knife**
- **¼ cup (60 ml) peanut butter**
- **2 cups (400 g) mixed variety birdseed**
- **paper plate**

❶ Spread out old newspapers to protect the surface on which you will be working.

❷ Tie a piece of string or yarn or wrap wire around the top of the pinecone.

❸ Use a Popsicle stick, plastic knife, or putty knife to spread peanut butter all over the pinecone.

❹ Pour birdseed onto the paper plate. Roll the pinecone in the birdseed until it is completely coated. You should not be able to see any peanut butter.

❺ Ask a grown-up to help you hang your bird feeder outside on the branch of a tree. Then watch the birds enjoy their special feast!

# Glossary

**Advent:** the Christian season beginning four Sundays before Christmas, when people prepare to celebrate the birth of Christ

**Aussies:** a nickname for Australians

**Aztecs:** the Native people who ruled the Mexican empire in the 1400s and early 1500s

**boisterous:** wild and noisy

**carp:** a freshwater fish commonly found in Asian countries

**caviar:** tiny, salted fish eggs that are prepared as food

**commemorates:** remembers and honors a person or a historic event with a ceremony or a celebration

**curds:** lumps of soured milk that are used to make cheese

**czar:** a Russian ruler similar to a king

**Declaration of Independence:** the written statement proclaiming the freedom of the United States from British rule

**fasting:** not eating or drinking for a certain period of time, especially as an act of religious devotion

**Hindu:** the main religion of India

**Islamic:** related to the Muslim religion founded by the prophet Muhammad

**knead:** to press, fold, and stretch dough with the hands

**Kyoto:** one of Japan's largest cities and the country's capital city from the ninth century to the mid-nineteenth century

**Lent:** forty days during the six weeks between Ash Wednesday and Easter, when Christians prepare to honor Christ's death and resurrection

**Mayan:** belonging to the great civilization of Native people who ruled in Central America from the third century to the ninth century

**neon:** very bright fluorescent lighting

**Pilgrims:** English immigrants who came to America in 1620 seeking religious freedom

**regatta:** a boat race or a series of boat races, especially sailing

**shrine:** a place devoted to one or more sacred or honored images

**venison:** deer meat that is used as food for humans

# More Books to Read

*Carnival*.  *A World of Holidays* (series).  Catherine Chambers (Raintree/Steck-Vaughn)

*Christmas in Mexico*.  *Christmas Around the World* (series). Cheryl L. Enderlein (Bridgestone Books)

*Cinco de Mayo*.  *A World of Holidays* (series).  Sarah Vázquez (Raintree/Steck-Vaughn)

*Crafts for Christmas*.  Kathy Ross (Millbrook Press)

*Festival Decorations*.  *Craft Workshop* (series).  Anne Civardi and Penny King (Crabtree)

*Festivals of the World* (series).  (Gareth Stevens)

*Hindu Festivals Cookbook*.  Kerena Marchant (Raintree/Steck-Vaughn)

# Web Sites

*Happy Chanukah!*
www.kidsdomain.com/holiday/chanukah/

*Happy Thanksgiving!*
www.kidsdomain.com/holiday/thanks/

*The Holiday Spot:  Holidays History*
www.theholidayspot.com/holiday_history.htm

*Holidays in Egypt*
www.horus.ics.org.eg/html/holidays_in_egypt.html

*Holidays on the net:  Holiday Celebrations*
www.holidays.net/index2.htm

# Index